THE BEGINNER GUITARIST

TABLE OF CONTENTS

page song

Guitar

1. Ode to Joy (Anthem of Europe)

L. V Beethoven

Arrangement & Transcription by Willy Espinoza

D A Bm E D A D

Joy, beau - ti - ful spark of gods, Daugh-ter of E - ly - si-um, We___ en - ter,

TAB

2 2 3 5 | 5 3 2 0 | 3 3 0 2 | 2 0 0 | 2 2 3 5

6

G D A D A D A D Em F♯

drunk with fi - re, Heaven-ly one, thy sanc - tua-ry! Your ma gic binds to - ge-ther what___ Cus-tom

6

5 3 2 0 | 3 3 0 2 | 0 3 3 | 0 2 3 | 0 2 3 2 3 | 0 2 3 2 0

12

Bm A D D7 G Gm (3fr.) D Em A D

strict - ly parted. All___ Men be - come___ Bro - thers, Where your gen - tle Wings a-bides.

12

3 0 2 | 2 2 3 5 | 5 3 2 0 | 3 3 0 2 | 0 3 3

Guitar

2. Brother John (Frère Jacques)

Traditional French Song

Arrangement & Transcription by Willy Espinoza

Guitar

3. Happy Birthday

Traditional

Arrangement & Transcription by Willy Espinoza

Guitar

4. This Land Is Your Land

Woody Guthrie

Arrangement & Transcription by Willy Espinoza

Guitar

5. I Saw Three Ships

The Chieftains

Arrangement & Transcription by Willy Espinoza

Guitar

6. Auld Lang Syne

Doguie McLean

Arrangement & Transcription by Willy Espinoza

Guitar

7. Amazing Grace

John Newton

Arrangement & Transcription by Willy Espinoza

Guitar

8. Aura Lee

W. W. Fosdick & George R. Poulton

Arrangement & Transcription by Willy Espinoza

Guitar

9. What Shall We Do with the Drunken Sailor

Traditional

Arrangement & Transcription by Willy Espinoza

Guitar

10. She'll Be Coming 'Round the Mountain

Traditional

Arrangement & Transcription by Willy Espinoza

2
10. She'll Be Coming 'Round the Mountain
C G7 C C
com - ming a-round the moun - tain when she comes. Sing - ing aye aye yip - pee yip - pee
G7 C F
aye Sing - ing aye aye yip - pee yip - pee aye Sing - ing aye aye yip - pee aye aye yip - pee
C G7 C
aye aye yip - pee yip - pee aye.

Guitar

11. Scotland The Brave

Traditional Scotland Song

Arrangement & Transcription by WIlly Espinoza

11. Scotland The Brave

Guitar

12. Kum Ba Yah

Traditional

Arrangement & Transcription by Willy Espinoza

Guitar

13. Die Gedanken sind frei

Traditional

Arrangement & Transcription by Willy Espinoza

Guitar

14. America The Beautiful

Music by Samuel A. Ward.
Lyrics by Katharine Lee Bates
Arrangement & Transcription by Willy Espinoza

Guitar

15. Tumbalalaika

Traditional

Arrangement & Transcription by Willy Espinoza

♩ = 120

Am E7

A young la - dy's think - ing think - ing all night Would it be wrong, he ask,

Am A7 Dm Am

or may - be right, Should he de - clare his love dare he choose, And would she a - ccept or

E7 Am E7 Am

will she re - fuse? Tum - ba - la, tum - ba - la, tum - ba - la - lai - ka tum - ba - la, tum - ba - la, tum - ba - la - lai - ka,

A7 Dm Am E7 Am

tum - ba - la - lai - ka play Ba - la - lai - ka, tum - ba - la - lai - ka Tum - ba - la - lai.

Guitar

16. My Bonnie Lies Over the Ocean

Guitar

17. Oh, My Darling, Clementine

Percy Montrose

Arrangement & Transcription by Willy Espinoza

Guitar

18. Banks of the Ohio

Traditional

Arrangement & Transcription by Willy Espinoza

Guitar

19. When the Saints Go Marching In

Traditional

Arrangement & Transcription by Willy Espinoza

Guitar

20. Wer ein Liebchen hat gefunden

Guitar

21. Theme from the New World Symphony

Antonin Dvorak

Arrangement & Transcription by Willy Espinoza

Guitar

22. For He's a Jolly Good Fellow

Traditional

Arrangement & Transcription by Willy Espinoza

Guitar

23. Spring

Antonio VIvaldi

Arrangement & Transcription by Willy Espinoza

23. Spring

E
B
16
20
24
29
tutti
f
p

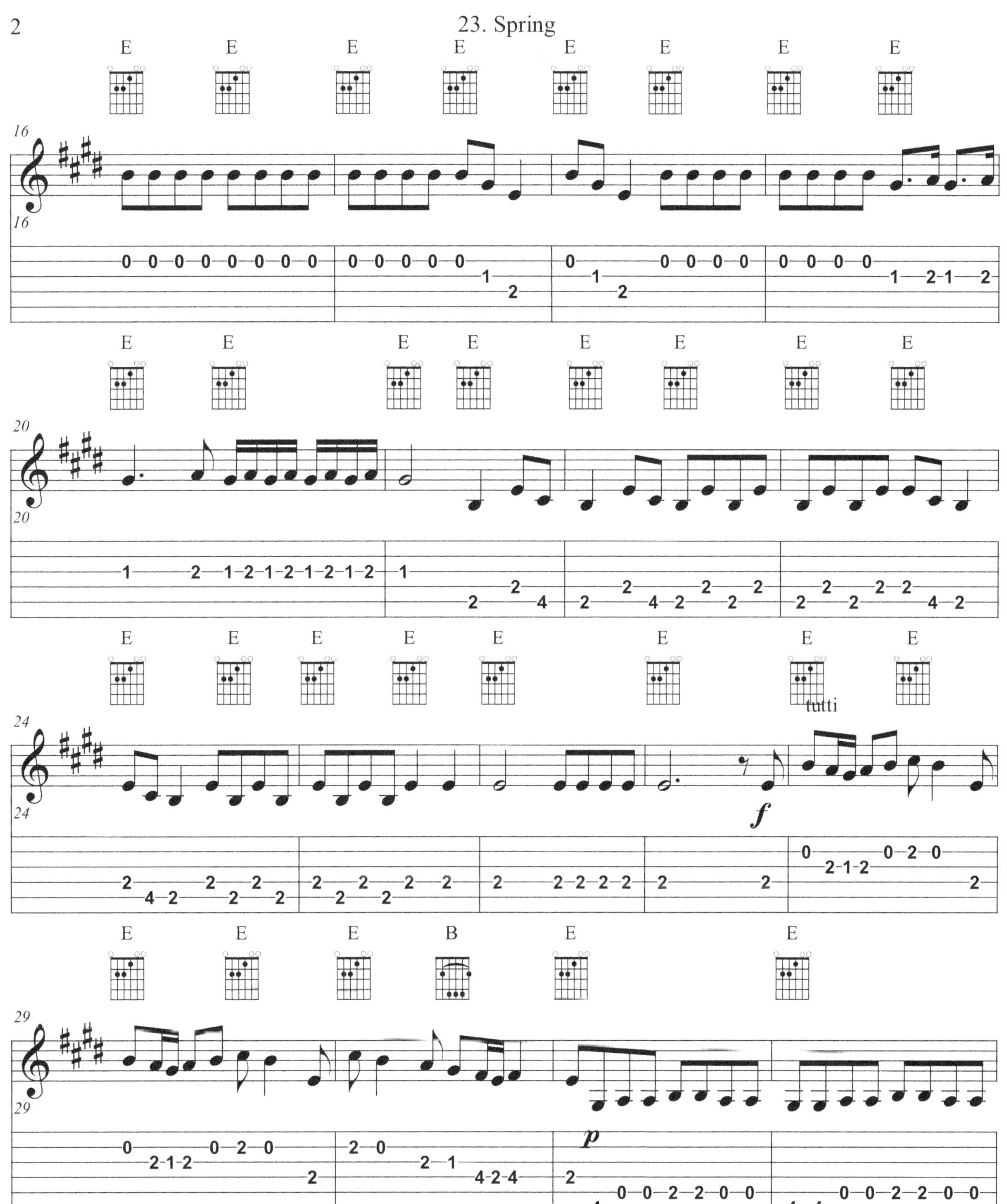

B
B
E
E
33
B
B
E
B
E
B
E
B
B
B
37
f
B
B
B
F♯7
B
42
Bm
Bm
E
E7
A
F♯
solo
45

23. Spring

F♯7 B G♯ G♯7 C♯m C♯m B6 A6 E B7
4fr. 4fr. 4fr. 4fr. 10fr.
C♯m C♯m G♯7 C♯m C♯m C♯m C♯m C♯m
tutti
mp
C♯m G♯7 C♯m Cm G♯
3fr.
solo
p
cresc.
C♯m C♯m C♯m C♯m C♯m C♯m

23. Spring
5
C♯m C♯m C♯m C♯m C♯m C♯m G♯ B E
4fr.
tutti
f
E E E E E B B
solo
mp
E A E A E E E B E E
tutti
f
E E E B E E E E
p
E E E B E

Guitar

24. 'O sole mio

Alfredo Mazzucchi & Eduardo di Capua

Arrangement & Transcription by Willy Espinoza

24. 'O sole mio

A
Bm
E7
Bm
17
Ma n'a - tu so - le cchiu' bel - lo, oi ne' 'O so - le mi - o
E7
A
A7
Dm
G7
A
23
sta nfron - te a te 'O so - le, 'O so - le, mi - o.
E7
A
A
29
1.
2.
sta nfron - te a te sta nfron - te a te. sta nfron - te a te.

Guitar

25. The Star-Spangled Banner

Francis Scott Key & John Stafford Smith

Arrangement & Transcription by Willy Espinoza

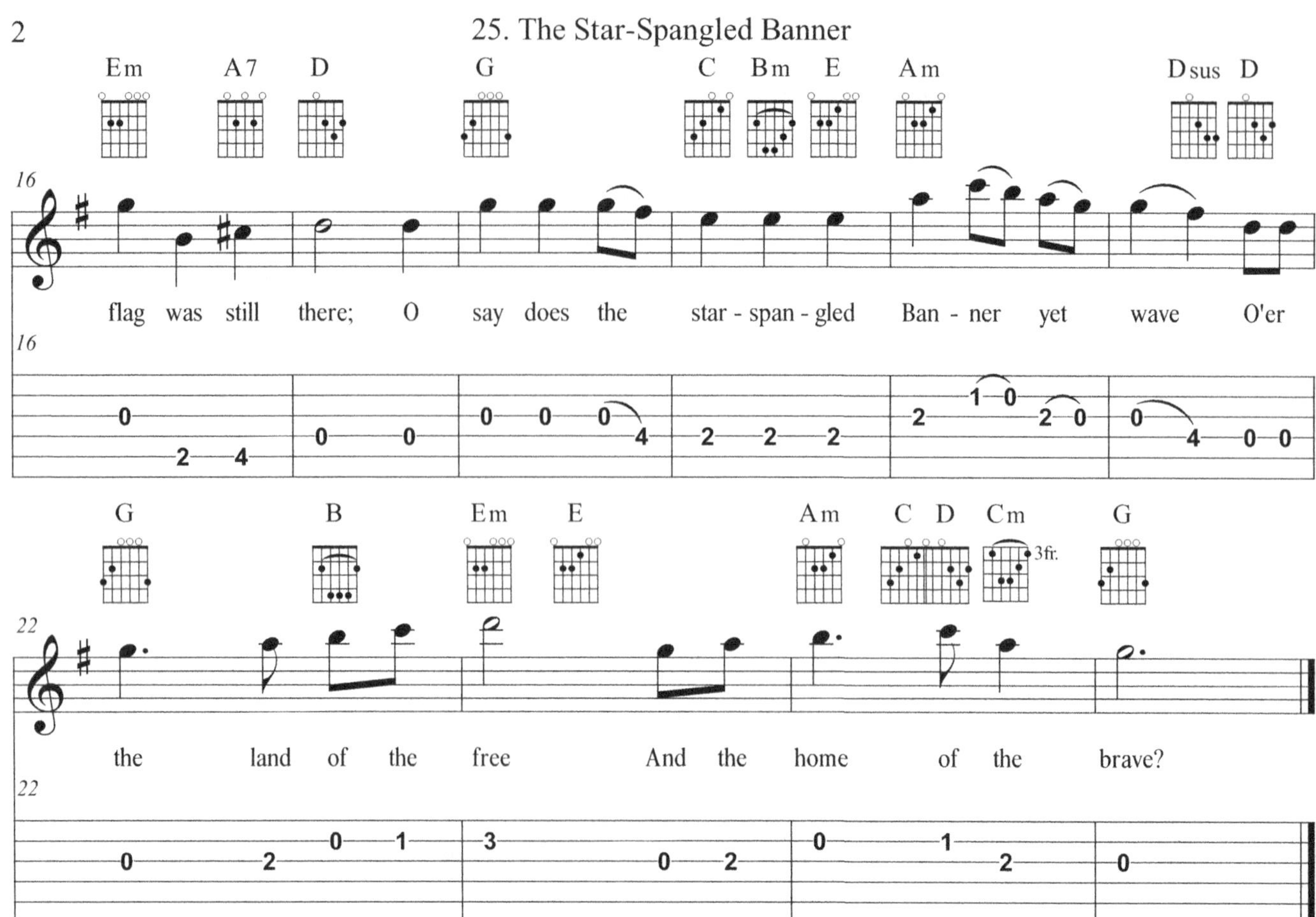
2
25. The Star-Spangled Banner
Em A7 D G C Bm E Am Dsus D
16
flag was still there; O say does the star - span - gled Ban - ner yet wave O'er
G B Em E Am C D Cm G
3fr.
22
the land of the free And the home of the brave?

Guitar

26. Sleeping Beauty Waltz

Piotr Ilich Tchaikovsky

Arrangement & Transcription by Willy Espinoza

Guitar

27. Wild Rover

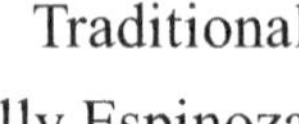

Traditional

Arrangement & Transcription by Willy Espinoza

♩ = 120

G C G

I've been a wild ro - ver for ma - ny's the year And I've spent all my
went to an ale-house I used to fre - quent And I told the land -

7

C D7 G C

mo - ney on whis - key and beer But now I'm re - tur - ning with gold in great
la - dy my mo - ney was spent I ask her for cre - dit, she ans - wered me

14

C G C D7 G D7

store And I ne - ver will play the wild ro - ver no more. And it's no, nay,
nay Such a cus - tum as yours I cad have a - ny day.

27. Wild Rover

Guitar

28. Can Can

Traditional

Arrangement & Transcription by Willy Espinoza

♩ = 160

D G D A7 D E7 A

9

D G D A7 D A7 D D

18

D A7 D D D A7 D D D

27

A7 D D D A7 D A7 D A7 D A7 D A7

D D D D D D D D G D7 G G
36
D7 G D7 G D7 G G D7
44
D7 G D7 G G D7 G
53
1.
2.

Guitar

29. Oh, Susanna!

Stephen Foster

Arrangement & Transcription by Willy Espinoza

Guitar

30. La donna è mobile

Guitar

31. Greensleeves

Traditional

Arrangement & Transcription by Willy Espinoza

Guitar

32. Habanera (Carmen)

Georges Bizet

Arrangement & Transcription by Willy Espinoza

D A7 A7 A7
mais, ja-mais con-un de loi, Si tu ne m'ai-mes pas, je t'al - me, Si je t'ai-me, prend garde a
D D D D A7 A7
toi. Si tu ne m'ai-me pas, si tu ne m'ai-mes pas, je t'aime Mais si je
f mp f mp
A7 A7 A D D D
t'ai - me, si je t'ai - me, prends garde a toi!!
f

Guitar

33. Minuet in G major

Wolfgang Amadeus Mozart

Arrangement & Transcription by Willy Espinoza

2
33. Minuet in G major
D
G
C
G
D7
18
18
C
G
D
G
24
24

34. God Save The Queen

Arrangement & Transcription by Willy Espinoza

Guitar

35. The Oak and the Ash

Mat Williams

Arrangement & Transcription by Willy Espinoza

Guitar

36. Toreador Song (Carmen)

Georges Bizet

Arrangement & Transcription by Willy Espinoza

2
36. Toreador Song (Carmen)
F Gm D7 Gm A♭ D Gm
Les spec-ta-teurs, per-dant la té-te, Les spec-ta-teurs s'in-ter-pel-lent á grand fra-cas!
Dm
A-pos-tro - phes, cris es ta-pas - ge Pous-sés jus-ques á la fu-reur!
Cm D Cm D Gm
Car c'est la fé-te du cou-ra - ge! C'est la fé - te desgend de coeur! Al-lons! en
D D G
gar-de! al-lons! al - lons! ah! Te-ré-a-dor, en gar - de!

36. Toreador Song (Carmen)
3
D G A D Am D7 G
To - ré - a-dor! To - ré - a-dor! Et son - ge bien, oui son - ge en com - bat - tant,
B F#7 Dm G
Qu'un oeil noir te re - gar - de Et que l'a - mour t'at - tend, To - ré - a - dor,
D7 D G G D G D G G
1. 2.
L'a - mour, l'a - mour t'at tend! tend! To - re - a - dor! l'a - mour t'at - tend! l'a -
G G G
mour t'at - tend!

Guitar

37. Bella Ciao

2
37. Bella Ciao
C7
Fm
16
l'om - bra di un bel fior.
0 1 0 1
3

Guitar

38. Tarantella Napoletana

Traditional

Arrangement & Transcription by Willy Espinoza

Dm
Dm
A7
Dm
Dm
Gm
3fr.
Dm
Gm
3fr.
Dm
A7
Dm
1.
A7
Dm
D
A7
2.
D

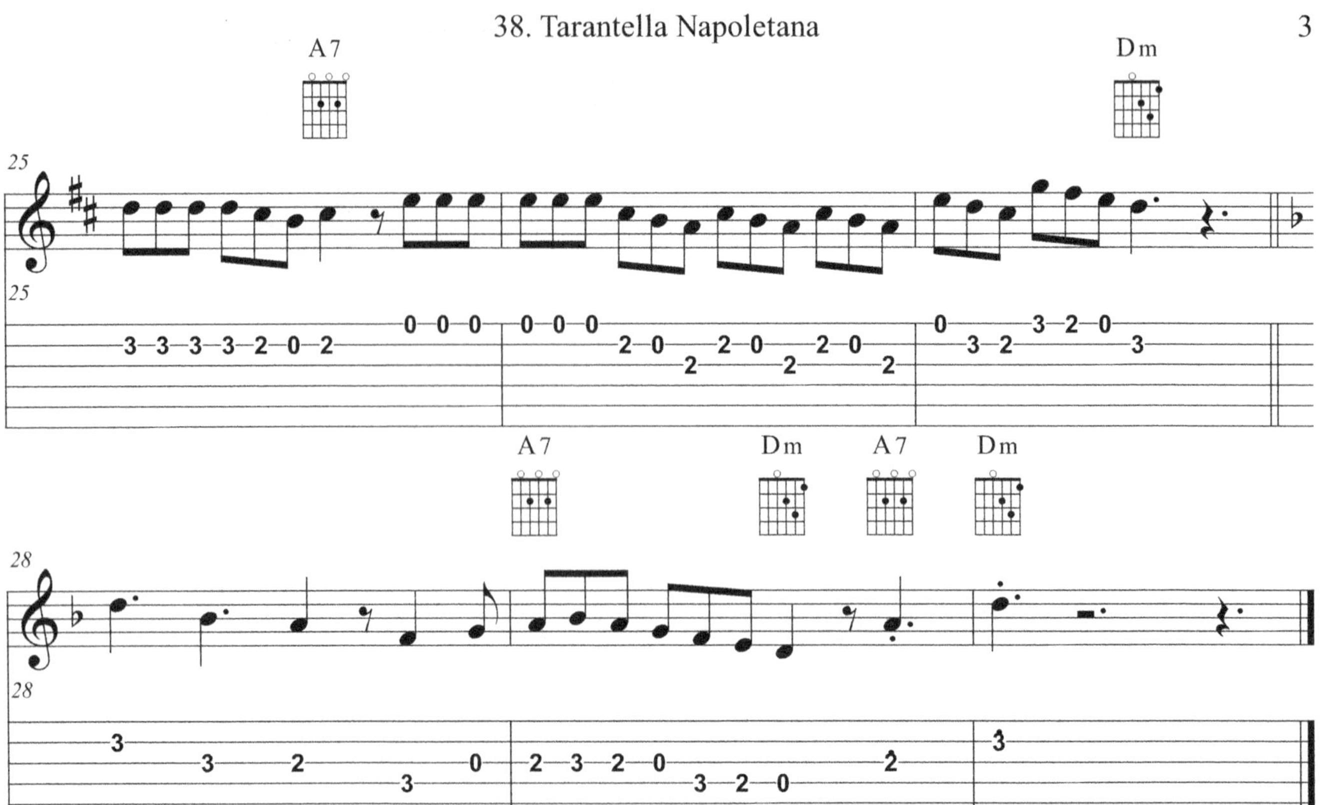
A7
Dm
25
A7
Dm
A7
Dm
28

Guitar

39. Minuet in D Minor

J.S. Bach

Arrangemet & Transcription by Willy Espinoza

Guitar

40. Eine kleine Nachtmusik

Wolfgang Amadeus Mozart

Arrangement & Transcription by Willy Espinoza

40. Eine kleine Nachtmusik
G A D A D A D
A A D G D
Bm A7 D G A D A7
D A D A

40. Eine kleine Nachtmusik
3
D B Em A7 D G D A D D A7
39
D Bm G D A7 D D
44
B C G
49
C G C E7
54

40. Eine kleine Nachtmusik

40. Eine kleine Nachtmusik

5

40. Eine kleine Nachtmusik

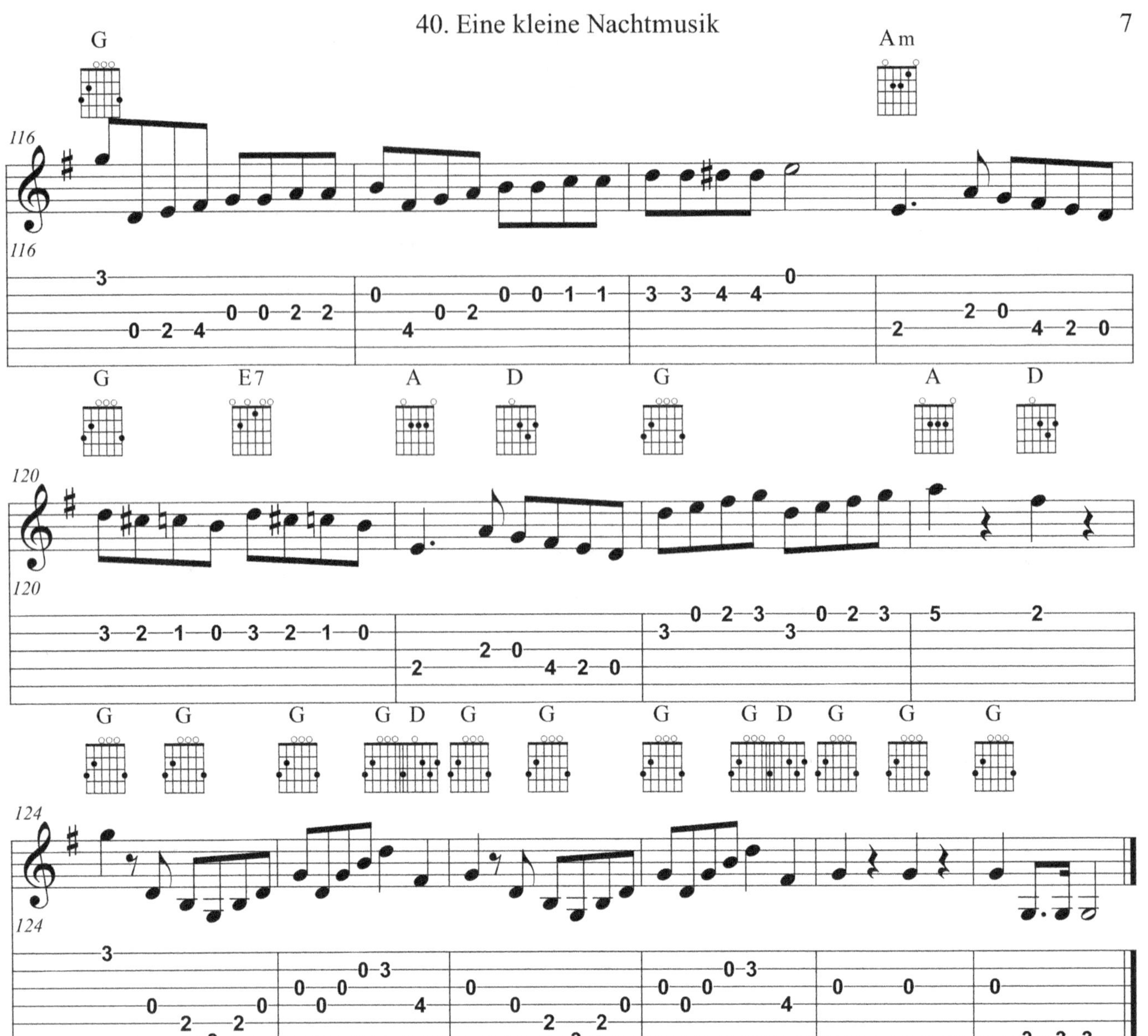
40. Eine kleine Nachtmusik
7
G
Am
116
G
E7
A
D
G
A
D
120
G
G
G
G
D
G
G
G
G
D
G
G
G
124

Guitar

41. Allegro in F major, K.lc

Wolfgang Amadeus Mozart

Arrangement & Transcription by Willy Espinoza

Guitar

42. Swan Lake

Piotr Ilich Tchaikovsky

Arrangement & Transcription by Willy Espinoza

Guitar

43. Wedding March

43. Wedding March

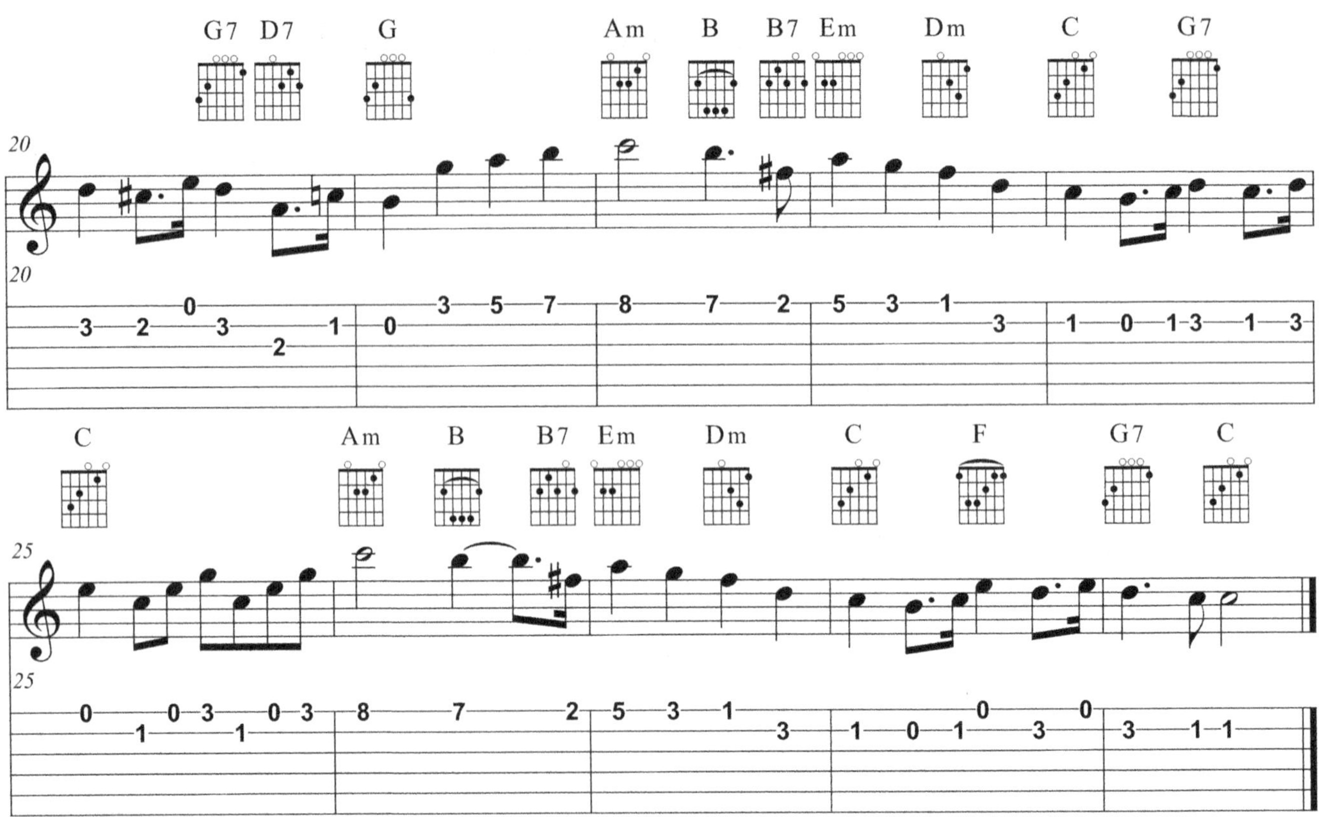

Guitar

44. Scarborough Fair

Simon & Garfunkel

Arrangement & Transcription by Willy Espinoza

Guitar

45. The Blue Danube

Johann Strauss

Arrangement & Transcription by Willy Espinoza

2
45. The Blue Danube
D
E
A
32
E
39
A
E7
A
1.
2.
A
46
D
A
53

45. The Blue Danube

Guitar

46. Für Elise

Ludwing Van Beethoven

Arrangement & Transcription by Willy Espinoza

2
46. Für Elise
Am
E
Am
E
Am
Fine
F
B♭
C
F
E7
Am
G
C
F
G
C
F
G
E7
E7
E7
D.S. al Fine

Guitar

47. Caprice No. 24.

Guitar

48. The Entertainer

Scott Joplin

Arrangement & Transcription by Willy Espinoza

C
C
C
F
Fine
1.
2.
C
C
B
G7
C
C
F
C
F
C
F
G7
C
C
Go To Measure 5
1.
2.

Guitar

49. The Swan (Le Cygne)

Camille Saint-Saëns

Arrangement & Transcription by Willy Espinoza

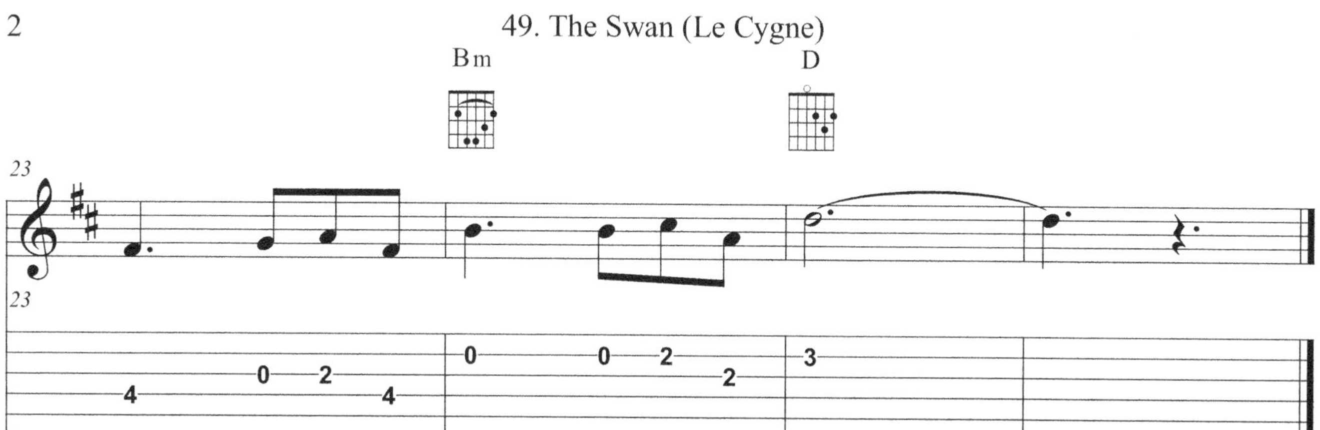
Bm
D
23
23
4
0
2
4
0
0
2
2
3

Guitar

50. March (The Nutcracker)

Piotr Ilich Tchaikovsky

Arrangement & Transcription by Willy Espinoza

♩ = 120

G Em G Em G Em G Em

5

Am D G Em B7 Em Am D

9

G Em G Em G Em G Em

13

Am D Bm Em Am D Em B

2

50. March (The Nutcracker)

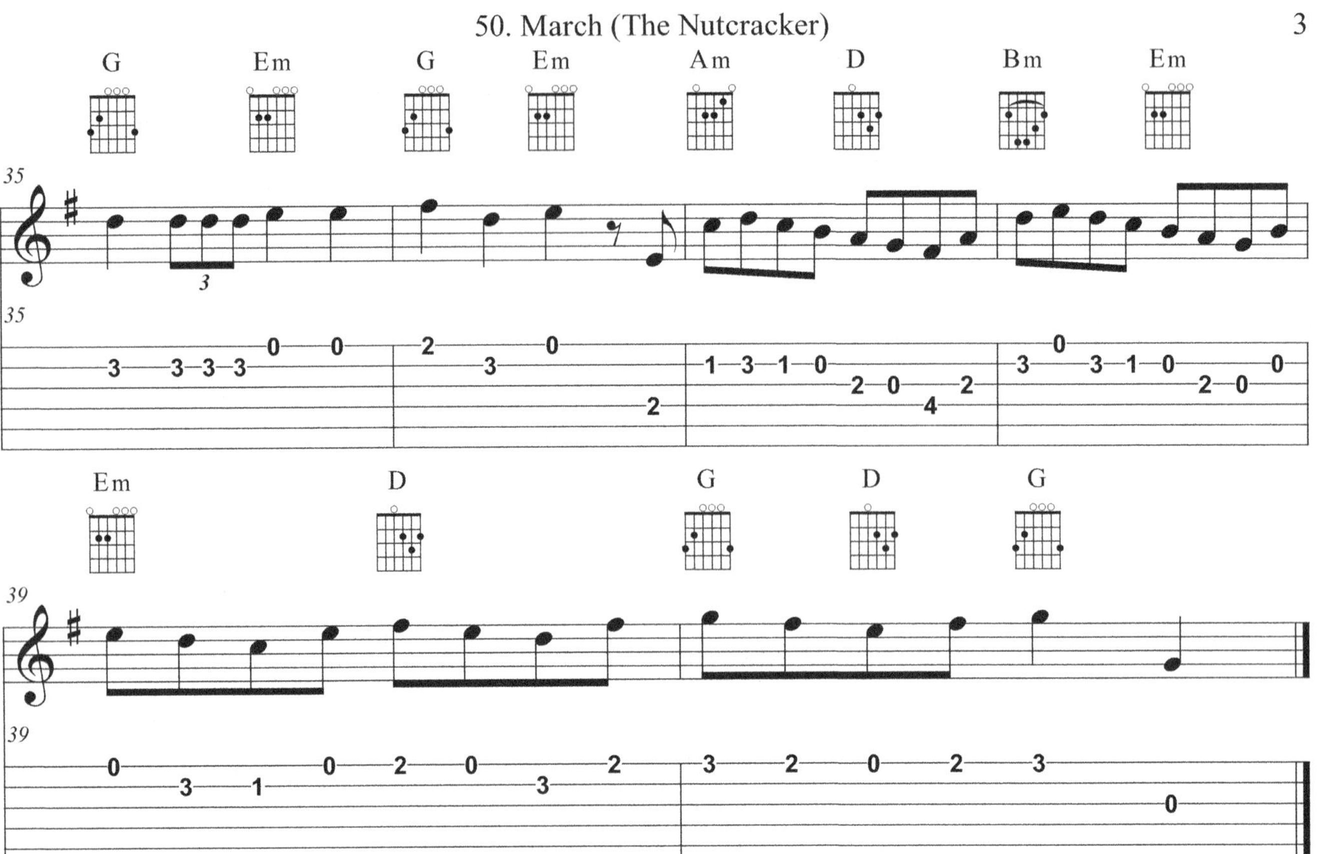
50. March (The Nutcracker)
3
G Em G Em Am D Bm Em
Em D G D G

Guitar

51. Der Hölle Rache (The Magic Flute)

Wolfgang Amadeus Mozart

Arrangement & Transcription by Willy Espinoza

51. Der Hölle Rache (The Magic Flute)
Cm A7 F B♭ F B♭
3fr.
so bist du mei - ne Toch - ter nim - mer - mehr, so bist mein' nein, mei - ne
B♭ F B♭ F Gm D
3fr.
Toch - terr nim - mer - mehr, ah ah
Gm B♭ F B♭ B♭ F B♭ B♭ F B♭
3fr.
1.
ah mei - ne
F B♭ B♭ C A7 Gm
3fr.
2.
Toch - ter nim - mer - mehr, ah so bist du mei - ne Toch - ter

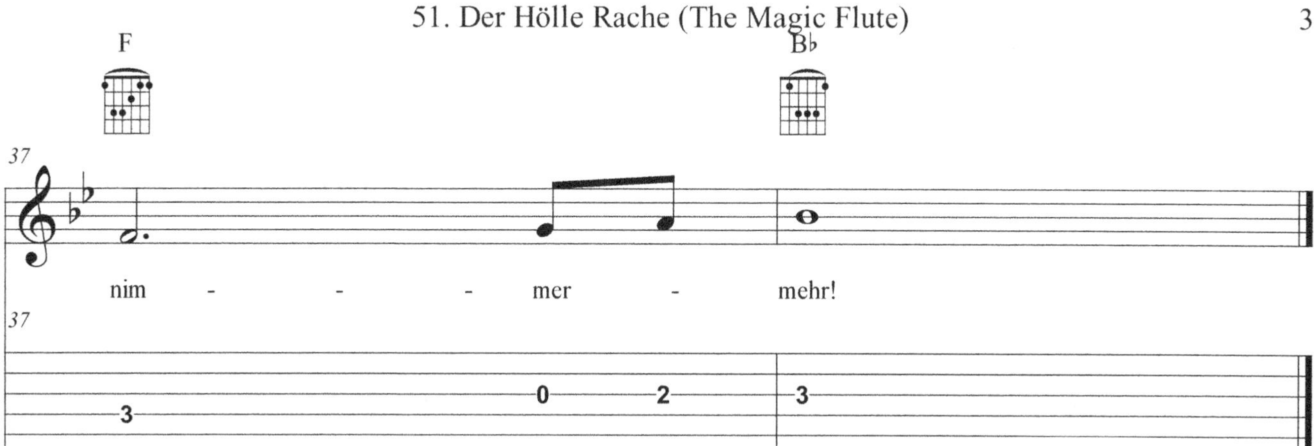
F
B♭
37
nim - - - mer - mehr!
37
3
0
2
3

Guitar

52. Symphony No. 40

(Great G minor symphony)

Wolfang Amadeus Mozart

Arrangement & Transcription by Willy Espinoza

2
52. Symphony No. 40
Cm
3fr.
F
B♭
Cm
3fr.
B♭
Cm
3fr.
B♭
C7
F
C7
F
C7

F
Gm
3fr.
Cm
3fr.
41
D7
Gm
3fr.
D7
46
Gm
3fr.
D7
Gm
3fr.
Gm
3fr.
D7
51
Gm
3fr.
57

52. Symphony No. 40

Guitar

53. Turkish March (Turkish Rondo)

Arrangement & Transcription by Willy Espinoza

Gm
3fr.
Gm
D7
Gm
Fine
12
12
6 5 3 2 3 3 4 1
3 2 0 3 5
G
D
G
G D G
G D G
D.S. al Fine
1.
2.
14
14
7 3 5 7 5 3 2 0 2 3 5 2 3 3 5 7 3 5 7 5 3 2 0 5 2 3 3 3 5
0 5 2 3 3 2 0 4 0

Guitar

54. Hungarian Dance No. 5

Johannes Brahms

Arrangement & Transcription by Willy Espinoza

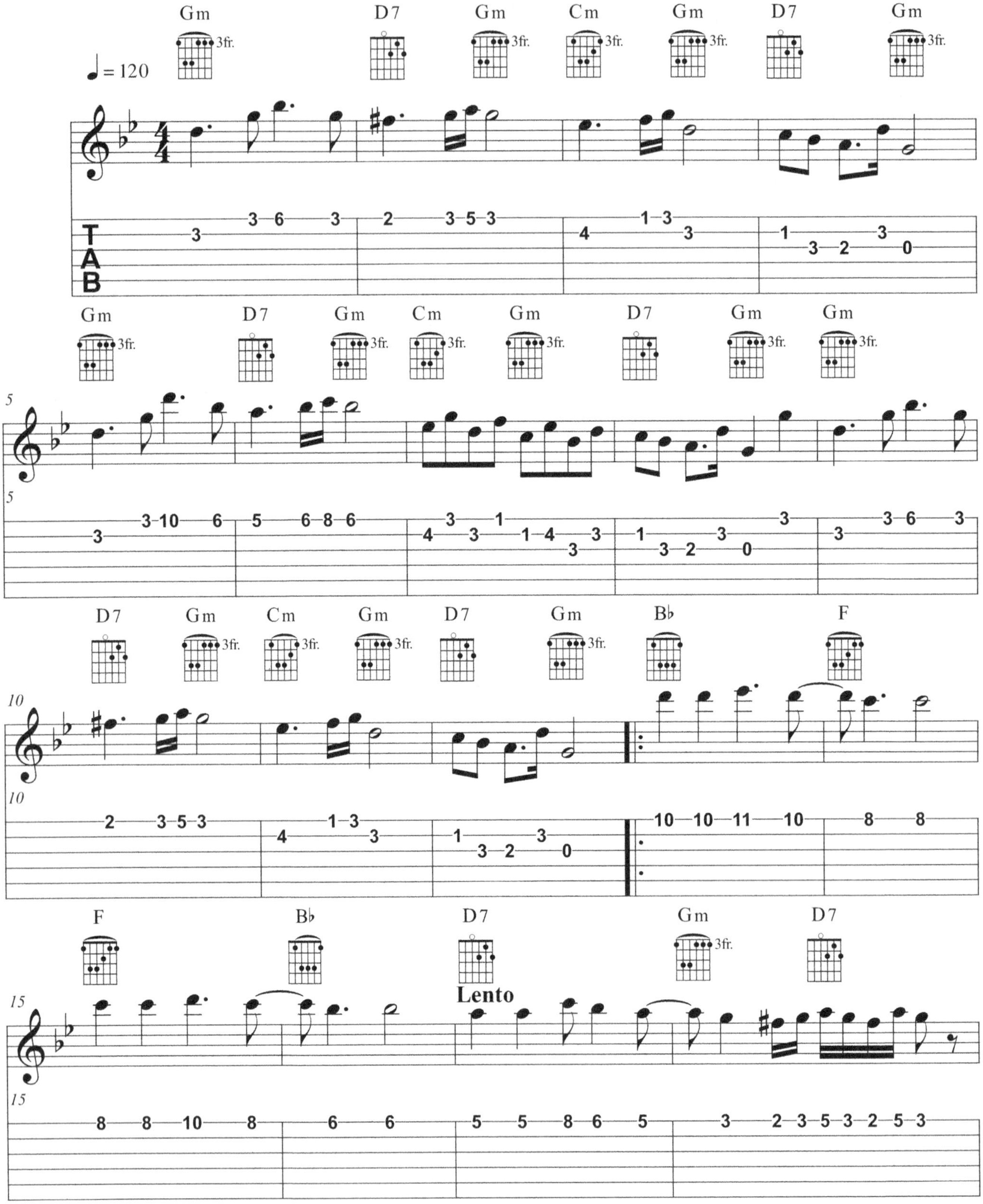
Gm D7 Gm Cm Gm D7 Gm
♩= 120
3fr.
TAB
Gm D7 Gm Cm Gm D7 Gm Gm
D7 Gm Cm Gm D7 Gm B♭ F
F B♭ D7 Gm D7
Lento

54. Hungarian Dance No. 5

Guitar

55. Adagio cantabile (Sonata Pathétique)

Ludwig van Beethoven

Arrangement & Transcription by Willy Espinoza

55. Adagio cantabile (Sonata Pathétique)

Guitar

56. Hickory Dickory Dock

Traditional

Arrangement & Transcription by Willy Espinoza

Guitar

57. The Camptown Races

Guitar

58. This Old Man

Traditional

Arrangement & Transcription by Willy Espinoza

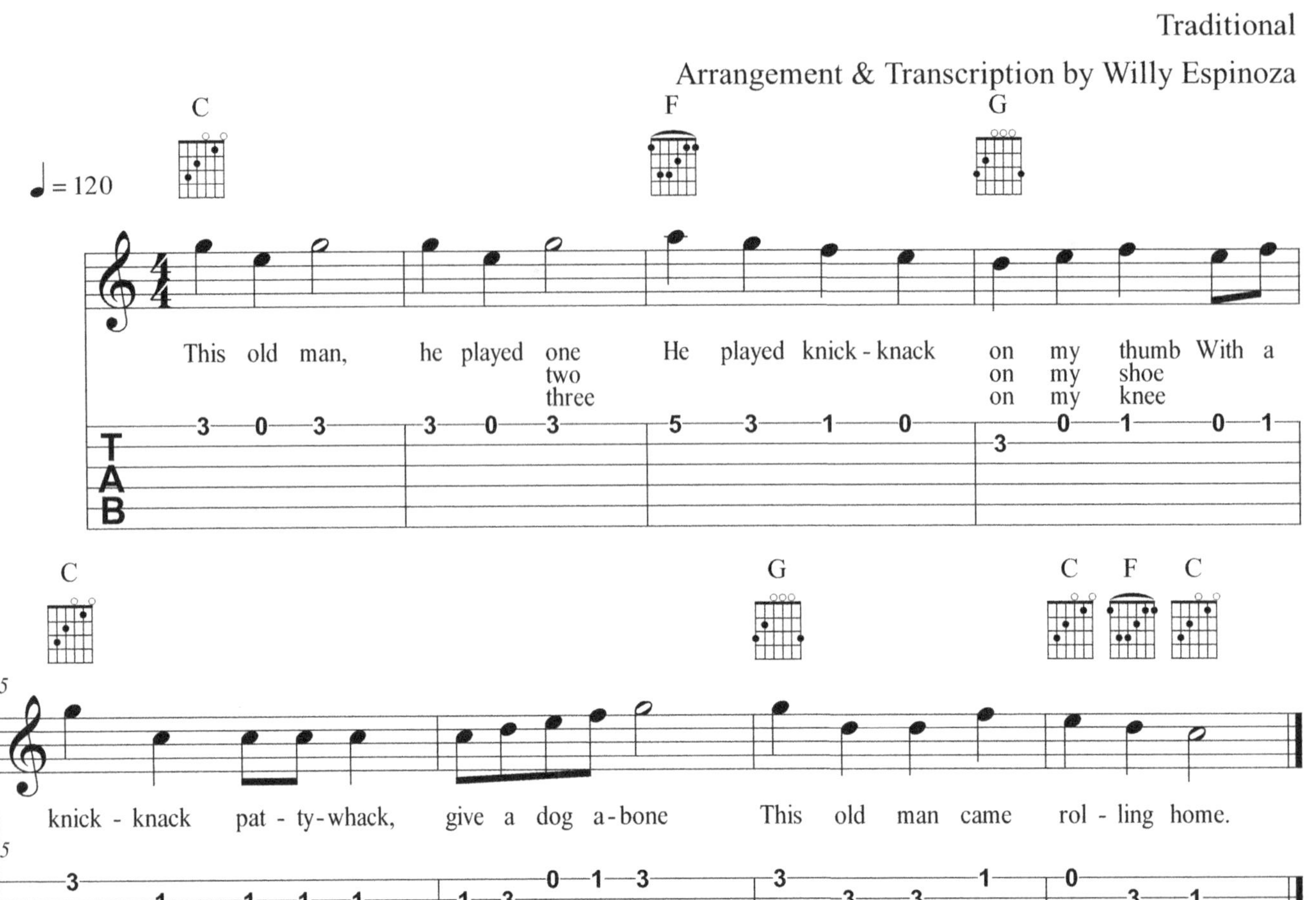

Guitar

59. O Holy Night

Adolphe Adam

Arrangement & Transcription by Willy Espinoza

59. O Holy Night

Guitar

60. Five Little Monkeys

Traditional

Arrangement & Transcription by Willy Espinoza

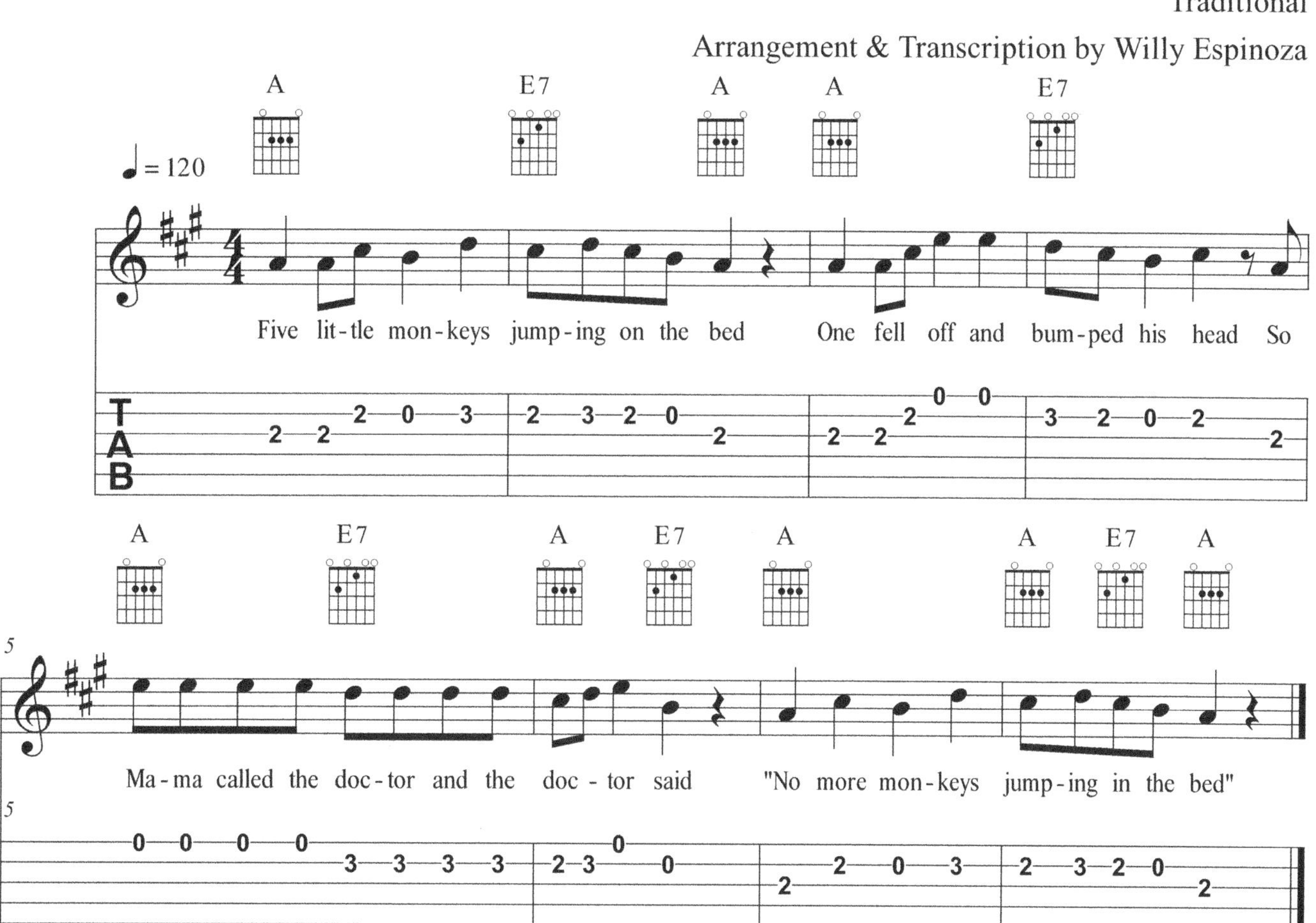

Made in the USA
Monee, IL
02 March 2026

45338967R00059